385·3610941

RHYTHMS OF STEAM

RHYTHMS OF STEAM

Images of the steam-age railway

Roger Siviter ARPS

•RAILWAY HERITAGE•
from
The NOSTALGIA *Collection*

First published in February 2000

British Library Cataloguing in Publication Data

A catalogue record for this book is available from the British Library.

ISBN 1 85794 140 3

Silver Link Publishing Ltd
The Trundle
Ringstead Road
Great Addington
Kettering
Northants NN14 4BW

Tel/Fax: 01536 330588
email: sales@slinkp-p.demon.co.uk

Printed and bound in Great Britain
by Butler & Tanner Ltd, Frome and London

Frontispiece On 4 March 1967 Ian Allan ran two special trains to commemorate the last day of through passenger services between Paddington and Birkenhead. They were hauled by ex-Great Western Railway (GWR) 'Castle' Class 4-6-0s Nos 4079 *Pendennis Castle* and No 7029 *Clun Castle*, by which time both were in private ownership. The second special, which was hauled by No 7029 between Banbury and Chester, is seen here just north of Cosford on the Wolverhampton to Shrewsbury leg of the journey. The train was named 'The Zulu' after the original GWR service that ran between Paddington and Birmingham via Didcot and Oxford in the 1880s. The route between Paddington and Banbury via High Wycombe and Bicester did not open until 1910.

Below The final year of British Railways (BR) steam working over the Settle & Carlisle route was 1967, and on 27 August of that year Class '5' 4-6-0 No 44911 coasts down the Mallerstang Valley near Soulby with an afternoon Leeds to Carlisle parcels train.

CONTENTS

ACKNOWLEDGEMENTS

For their help in compiling this book I would like to thank my publisher, Silver Link, Tim Hall, Christina Siviter, and all railwaymen, professional and amateur, who made it all possible.

Unless otherwise stated, all pictures were taken by the author.

INTRODUCTION

AT FIRST GLANCE the title *Rhythms of Steam* may seem rather a strange one in relation to railways. But is it? The dictionary definition of 'rhythm' is 'movement with regular succession', and I think that this can be well applied to train sounds, particularly in the era of steam traction. Having been a professional musician for most of my life, playing all styles of music from Bach to Bebop, I find a great affinity between the rhythms of music, whether it be classical or jazz, and the wonderful sounds of steam locomotives at work. And I am not alone in this, for I find that many of my musician friends are also intoxicated by railways.

Over the years many great musicians were influenced by railways, including the Swiss composer Arthur Honegger, who composed 'Pacific 231', and the celebrated American jazz musician and composer Gerry Mulligan (his father was a locomotive engineer), who composed a jazz piece entitled 'Flying Scotsman'. Moreover, it was always said that the great boogie-woogie pianists of the 1920s, Pine Top Smith, Meade Lux Lewis, et al, were inspired by the sounds of American freight trains, hence the famous 'Honky Tonk Train Blues'.

It is a fairly well-known fact that the two professions in which the most railway enthusiasts are to be found are the church and music. I can't vouch for the former (although many years ago when, as was the style of the day, I used to sign my pictures with my full initials R. E. B. Siviter, someone mistakenly addressed me as the Reverend

Siviter!) but I do know that there is a definite link between music and railways, and in particular the 'Rhythms of Steam'.

This book is set out in eight sections to show the many different aspects of steam at work. You will also notice one section called 'Diesel invasion', and may think it odd in a book on steam. However, I am sure that many of you, like myself, maybe regret not taking more pictures of the 'invaders' when steam was declining, as all the infrastructure was still the same even though the traction was changing; I therefore look on this section as a catalyst for the future. Finally, I hope that through these eight sections I will convey to you, the reader, something of the varied 'Rhythms of Steam'.

I have used in the book many colour and a few black and white prints taken by my friend and fellow musician Ken Blocksidge. Ken and myself went out on many trips together, but tragically he died of cancer at the age of only 37. He was diagnosed with the disease in the summer of 1971, and our last trip together was to see *King George V* on the 'Return to Steam' train at Bentley Heath near Solihull on 2 October of that year. He died the next day. His mum entrusted me with his picture collection, and as I was standing beside him when he took most of the pictures, I am able to write about them with some knowledge, and of course they bring back memories of the many good times spent together, both on the lineside and when we played together in bands, and would talk endlessly about steam and jazz.

Opposite A few miles west of the Settle & Carlisle route is the West Coast Main Line (WCML), and these two pictures were taken at Low Gill, just south of Tebay, on 31 August 1967. The first shows a down Carlisle goods train hauled by 'Black Five' 4-6-0 No 44775; note the metal milk churns in the foreground. The second picture shows the rear of a southbound works train, hauled by BR Standard Class '4MT' 4-6-0 No 75030. Anyone visiting this location today will find most of the area on the right-hand side of the picture now filled with the M6 motorway and, of course, electric catenary running above the railway tracks.

Early days in West Wales: during a family holiday to Tenby in August 1951,
I managed to take a few pictures during my train-spotting forays in the area. In the first
ex-GWR '8100' Class 2-6-2 tank No 8102 heads west out of Tenby with a mixed freight
train, including a tank wagon. The second photograph shows 2-6-0 No 4358,
shedded at Whitland (87H), pausing at Tenby station with an up express.

1. GOODS TRAINS

Above Steam working finished on British Railways (BR) in August 1968, and by the spring of that year it was confined to the North West of England, mainly round the Manchester and Preston areas. One of the routes that saw steam activity right until the end was the line from Preston to Blackburn and Burnley, and on 6 June 1968 ex-LMS '8F' 2-8-0 No 48191 climbs the 1 in 101 gradient at Long Barn near Hoghton with a lengthy train of coal empties bound for the Blackburn area.

Right It is 5.30am on 26 May 1966, and Class '5' 4-6-0 No 44694 is seen south of York station with a northbound freight train. I had been playing on a jazz gig in Birmingham the previous evening, and with my good friend, fellow musician and mad-keen railway enthusiast Mike Burney, had travelled to York overnight in order to get in a full day's 'photting', hence the early start! By the way, the picture was taken at 125th of a second at f1.8.

Opposite On 25 April 1968 '8F' No 48118 was photographed at Skelton Junction, formerly part of the Cheshire Lines Committee (CLC) system, with a Widnes to Stockport coal train. This train had run via the London & North Western Railway (LNWR) route from Widnes, the CLC line to Widnes being the centre one of the three converging lines. The line on the right, also CLC, runs back under the other two lines and heads south to Northwich. Note the unusual signal box and also the height of the signal of the right, both obviously so constructed for sighting purposes.

Turning round from the previous scene we see No 48118 as it pulls away from Skelton Junction towards Stockport.

Above Another '8F' 2-8-0, this time No 48410, heads out of Stourbridge Junction on the afternoon of 5 July 1966 with a southbound goods train for the Kidderminster area.

Right until the closure of Stourbridge shed in July 1966 and Tyseley in November 1966, there was still had an allocation of ex-GWR 0-6-0 pannier tanks for local trip working and shunting on the lines around Stourbridge. These next three pictures show the panniers at work in the area.

The first scene shows 0-6-0 pannier tank No 9608 climbing out of Stourbridge on the line to Wolverhampton with a train of mainly empty wagons on 4 July 1966.

On 26 September 1966, the date of the second view, No 4696 climbs the steep grade out of Halesowen towards Old Hill with the daily Halesowen to Stourbridge goods train, with Class '2MT' 2-6-0 No 46442 acting as banker. This train was probably the last regular working for the panniers on BR.

The final picture shows No 4646 running bunker-first banking a goods train off the Halesowen branch into Old Hill station on 9 September 1966. Once the train has gained the main line No 4646 will take it forward to Stourbridge Junction.

A memory of the former Great Central Railway, as Class '5' 4-6-0 No 45289 hurries out of Catesby Tunnel near Charwelton with a southbound empty newspaper/van train, probably the 10.57am Nottingham to Neasden Sidings, on the early afternoon of 13 August 1966. Ken Blocksidge and myself had travelled to this location to see unrebuilt Bulleid 'West Country' 'Pacific' 4-6-2 No 34002 on an RCTS Great Central railtour (see the picture on page 67), and we were rewarded with this bonus picture. Note the family group on the left-hand side. *Ken Blocksidge, Roger Siviter collection*

Ex-London Midland & Scottish Railway (LMS) 4-6-0 No 44775 runs through Low Gill with a Carlisle-bound goods train on 31 August 1967. (See also the picture on page 6.)

Left Steam on the East Coast Main Line (ECML): ex-London & North Eastern Railway (LNER) 'B1' Class 4-6-0 No 61337 makes steady progress along the four-track section near Copmanthorpe, just south of York, with an up coal train on 21 September 1966.

Below The former North Eastern Railway 0-8-0s (LNER Class 'Q6') lasted until the end of steam in the North East in September 1967. No 63459 of this famous class is seen near Gateshead shed with a scrap-metal train on 31 March 1966.

On 23 August 1966 BR Standard Class '9F' 2-10-0 No 92107 was photographed near Mollington
on the Birkenhead-Chester line with an up goods train. Steam remained active on this route until the end of the
Paddington-Birkenhead through service in March 1967.

Above 'Black Five' 4-6-0 No 44899 heads an eastbound rail train near Hoghton on the Preston-Blackburn line on 18 April 1968.

Right Steam on the Cambrian lines in mid-Wales survived until March 1967, mainly on passenger workings, especially on the summer Saturday holiday trains. It therefore came as something of a surprise, at midday on Saturday 20 August 1966, to see ex-LMS Class '2MT' 2-6-0 No 46446 and a brake-van heading down Talerddig bank towards Machynlleth, possibly after a morning's shunting work at Caersws or Newtown, or even both.

Scout Green, 5 miles north of Tebay on the WCML, had always been a popular spot with enthusiasts, and never more so than during the final years of steam working over the 1 in 75 of Shap incline. In addition, most freight trains were banked by steam locomotives for the 5 miles from Tebay to Shap summit, which added to the visual and aural excitement.

In the first photograph, taken on 25 June 1966, BR Standard 'Britannia' Class 'Pacific' No 70040 (formerly *Clive of India*) seems to be letting the banking engine – ex-LMS Fairburn 2-6-4 tank No 42251 – do most of the work as it approaches Scout Green signal box with a train of flat wagons bound for Carlisle.

The other two views show another 'Britannia', No 70035 *Rudyard Kipling*, labouring past Scout Green signal box on 30 August 1967 with a heavy northbound coal train. This train had just re-started after pausing for a 'blow-up' (to restore sufficient steam pressure) a few yards to the south. It was banked by BR Standard Class '4MT' 4-6-0 No 75037, seen in the third photograph about to pass the diminutive signal box.

Left On a murky 18 November 1967 'Black Five' 4-6-0 No 44887 climbs through Newton Heath with a coal train bound for Todmorden and the West Riding. On the left-hand side is the edge of Newton Heath shed.

Above Ex-LMS 4-6-0 No 45302 approaches Cosford with a midday Shrewsbury to Wolverhampton parcels train on 26 January 1967.

Below Although steam had declined by 1966, there was still a fair amount of activity around the West Riding of Yorkshire, especially on freight workings. On 12 July 1966 ex-LMS Ivatt Class '4MT' 2-6-0 No 43125 is seen with a northbound goods train near Normanton. These sturdy 2-6-0s were regarded as rather ugly looking when they were introduced in 1947, and were given the nickname 'Pigs'. Happily, one is preserved at the Severn Valley Railway.

In the latter days of steam on BR the WCML at Low Gill always seemed to me to be one of the ideal places at which to see steam still at work, for even in the last year of steam here, 1967, there was still quite a lot of activity, with a variety of locomotive classes to be seen: '8F' 2-8-0s, 'Black Five' 4-6-0s and ex-LMS 2-6-0s, as well as a variety of BR Standard classes including '9F' 2-10-0s, 'Britannia' 'Pacifics', '4MT' 4-6-0s and 2-6-0s. In the first photograph, taken on 31 August 1967, 'Britannia' No 70014 *Iron Duke* heads north with a ballast train.

Two days earlier, BR Standard Class '9F' 2-10-0 No 92125 hurries through Low Gill with an afternoon down goods, while a few minutes earlier BR Standard Class '4MT' 4-6-0 No 75026 heads south for Carnforth with a works train. This last view clearly shows the trackbed of the old LNWR/Midland Railway line from Clapham Junction (Yorks), which joined the WCML at Low Gill. Out of sight off the right-hand side of the picture (on the line to Clapham) is a viaduct that is still there today.

There are not many locations where you can photograph trains against a backdrop of a mediaeval castle, but one of the most famous is Conway Castle, situated alongside the North Wales coast route of the Chester to Holyhead line. At 5.40pm on 5 September 1966 Class '5' 4-6-0 No 45279 heads for Chester with a mixed goods train, while a few minutes earlier, at 5.30pm, another 'Black Five', this time No 45345, had passed with a fitted freight train bound for Holyhead.

Above One of the joys of chasing steam in its final few years was finding branch lines that were still open, such as the Cromford & High Peak line in Derbyshire. This quarry line, which included the famous 1 in 14 Hopton Incline, lasted until April 1967, using ex-LMS 0-4-0 tank locomotives and ex-LNER (War Department) saddle tanks. One of the latter, Class 'J94' 0-6-0 saddle tank No 68006, works back to Middleton with empties from Parsley Hay on 20 May 1966. The location is near Newhaven Farm crossing, on the A5012 Cromford to Newhaven road.

Above right Early morning at Long Barn (near Hoghton) on the Preston-Blackburn line: Class '5' 4-6-0 No 45436 heads for Blackburn with a van train from the Preston area on 27 February 1968.

Right On 11 July 1966 BR Standard Class '4MT' 4-6-0 No 75058 trundles downgrade near Gargrave with a Hellifield to Skipton goods train.

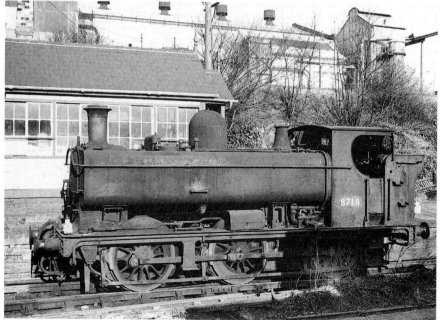

Although the Halesowen to Longbridge line closed in 1963, the section from Halesowen to Old Hill (on the Birmingham to Stourbridge Junction route) remained open until 1969, with daily steam working until the closure of Tyseley shed in November 1966.

In the first picture, taken on 2 June 1966, ex-GWR Class '3F' 0-6-0PT No 9774 takes water at the southern end of Halesowen station. This short spur to the water tower was all that remained of the former Midland line to Longbridge (and the Birmingham-Bristol main line).

Regular passenger services had finished on the branch in the 1920s, but the Austin workmen's train ran until 1953, so the station and its surroundings remained more or less intact until closure. In the second photograph ex-GWR pannier tank No 8718 pauses between shunting duties by the signal box, situated on the southbound platform, on 12 March 1966.

To serve the local steel works a daily freight ran from Halesowen to Stourbridge Junction, which necessitated being banked up the steep incline to Old Hill. On 3 October 1966 ex-LMS Class '2MT' 2-6-0 No 46470 banks a heavy goods train for Stourbridge, hauled by pannier tank No 9774. The location is just south of Old Hill Tunnel.

Above Just north of Oxenholme on the WCML is Grayrigg bank, 6 miles at a gradient of around 1 in 120. In steam days it was an ideal place to watch and photograph northbound trains, and on 16 September 1966, just north of Oxenholme, 'Britannia' 'Pacific' No 70051 *Firth of Forth* was photographed heading for Carlisle with a van train. Note the ornate road bridge.

Right On the late evening of the previous day the camera caught '9F' 2-10-0 No 92208 as it neared the summit of Grayrigg bank with a heavy coal train.

We finish this section on freight trains with four views of the popular BR Standard Class '9F' 2-10-0s at work. These locomotives were first introduced in 1954, and were built over a period of six years, No 92220 being the last steam locomotive to be built by BR, in March 1960. This honour went to the former GWR Works at Swindon, and the locomotive was appropriately named *Evening Star* after former GWR locomotives that had included the 'Star' Class 4-6-0 No 4002. The name was chosen as a result of a competition in the Western Region's staff magazine. This locomotive, together with five other members of this illustrious class, have been preserved, including No 92203, acquired by the railway and wildlife artist David Shepherd, and named *Black Prince*.

In the first photograph a grimy looking No 92135 heads through Water Orton with a coal train for the Birmingham area from the Leicestershire coalfields on 21 May 1966. The next view shows No 92212 heading down Hatton bank on the evening of 29 July 1966 with a train of Minis from Longbridge to Southampton Docks. Happily, the Mini is still being made at Longbridge, and 1999 saw the 40th anniversary of this very popular car.

A more mundane duty for No 92247 is illustrated by the third photograph as it runs down Hatton bank with an empty ore train bound for the Banbury area on 25 July 1966.

The '9Fs' lasted almost to the end of BR steam, and one of the last to be withdrawn, in May 1968, was No 92118, seen in the final picture shunting at the Furness yard at Carnforth on 17 April 1968, only a few weeks before withdrawal. This locomotive was built in 1956, so it only had a working life of just 12 years, a short span for a steam locomotive.

2. LARGE STATIONS

Large stations have always fascinated me and none more so than Manchester Victoria (and Exchange), where in steam days there always seemed to be a locomotive lurking among its many platforms. This was certainly the case on the very murky morning of 18 November 1967, as 'Britannia' 'Pacific' No 70035 (formerly *Rudyard Kipling*) pauses in one of the bay platforms between shunting duties.

Earlier that morning No 45017 was photographed arriving at Victoria with the 6.15am parcels train from Heysham.

Left Apart from the pleasure of finding locomotives, large stations always seemed to be wonderful conveyors of the sounds of steam, which would echo off the high roofs, especially on a cold winter's day like 9 March 1968 at Manchester Victoria, where 4-6-0 No 44851 is busying itself shunting a parcels train.

Right Around all large stations there were shunting duties, with empty stock trains and parcels trains to be made up. Here No 45255 shunts a parcels train by Manchester Victoria's East Junction signal box on 17 July 1966. The lines veering to the left are to Cheetham Hill, while straight ahead is up Miles Platting bank and on to Stalybridge and Leeds to the east, and Rochdale and Todmorden to the north.

Below Only four 'Black Five' 4-6-0s were named, including No 45156 *Ayrshire Yeomanry*, seen here shunting empty stock at the eastern end of Victoria station on 1 June 1968, a few weeks before the end of steam on BR.

Above No 70035 again (see page 37), this time shunting in the fog near the East Junction signal box at Manchester Victoria on 18 November 1967.

Left Manchester Victoria, with its 17 platforms, is obviously much larger than the adjoining Exchange station with only five, but connecting them is the longest platform in the country, 2,194 feet in length. Although it is known as No 11, it actually comprises Victoria's No 11, No 11 Middle (which joins Victoria to Exchange), and Exchange's No 3. The first of the BR Standard Class '5MT' 4-6-0s, No 73000, shunts vans at platform 2 of Exchange station on 9 March 1968. This is one of the two terminal platforms, the other three all being through platforms.

Right On the same day '8F' 2-8-0 No 48678 runs by the side of platform 4 at Exchange station with an eastbound goods. The platform from which the picture was taken is number 3, part of the long one linking the two stations.

We now leave the Red Rose county (in those days Manchester was in Lancashire) and visit the Roman city of York and its beautiful station. The first view, looking south, shows BR Standard Class '3MT' 2-6-0 No 77012 and an ex-GWR signal inspection coach waiting to depart to Darlington on the morning of 26 May 1966.

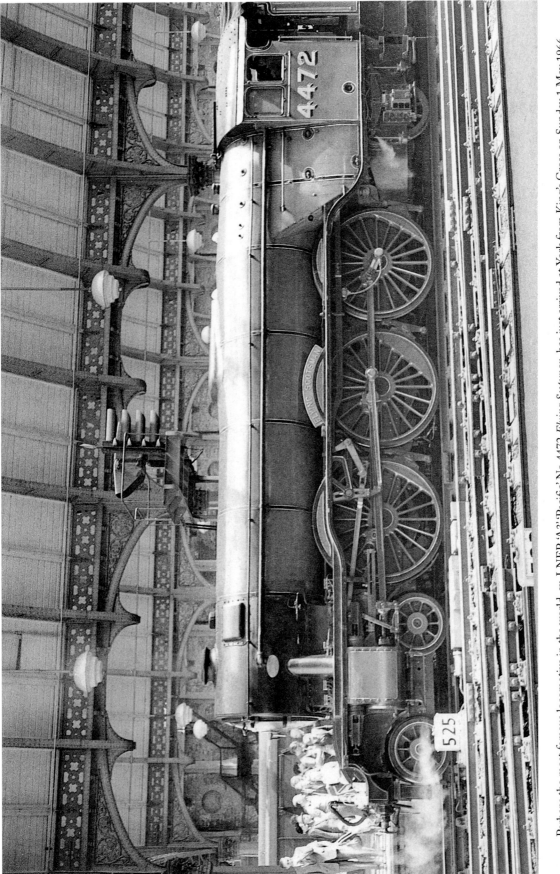

Perhaps the most famous locomotive in the world, ex-LNER 'A3' 'Pacific' No 4472 *Flying Scotsman*, has just arrived at York from King's Cross on Sunday 1 May 1966 with a special charter train, appropriately called the 'White Rose'. This view gives some idea of the beauty of the station's overall roof.

The last main-line terminus station in London to see regular steam working was the former Southern Railway station at Waterloo, where right until the end of Southern steam in July 1967 tank engines could be found on station pilot duties. This was certainly the case on 5 June 1967, as confirmed by these two views of BR Standard Class '4MT' 2-6-4T No 80015. A number of these fine locomotives have been preserved and today can often be found (sometimes in tandem) working special charter trains on the main line.

The reason I was at Waterloo on this day was that I was playing at a gig with the Andy Ross Band at the Hammersmith Palais that night and, instead of coming to London from Birmingham on the band coach, I and fellow trumpeter Don Morgan decided to take an early train from New Street and hopefully see a few steam workings at Waterloo, knowing full well that it was all due to finish on 9 July. I was hoping to see one of the ex-SR 'Pacifics', and I was not disappointed, for when I arrived at Waterloo 'Battle of Britain' Class 'Pacific' No 34090 (formerly *Sir Eustace Missenden, Southern Railway*) was at one of the arrival platforms with a train from Bournemouth. Next to the steam locomotive was 'Warship' Class diesel-hydraulic No D827 *Kelly*, which had just arrived with a morning train from Exeter.

Above and above right Some of the large stations that I visited in steam days have now closed, including Leeds Central and Nottingham Victoria. In the early spring of 1966 Ken Blocksidge and myself spent a week in the North of England photographing steam, and we visited Leeds Central on a snowy 2 April 1966, where Ken took these pictures of Stanier 2-6-4 tank No 42689 and Fairburn 2-6-4 tank No 42073 shunting. The station closed on 1 May 1967. *Both Ken Blocksidge, Roger Siviter collection*

Right On 1 September 1966 '8F' 2-8-0 No 48212 heads through Nottingham Victoria station with a northbound coal train. Beyond the signal box is the entrance to Mansfield Road Tunnel. Through services between Nottingham Victoria and London Marylebone finished on 3 September 1966 and the station closed shortly afterwards. The area is now a shopping centre, although the clock tower remains as a reminder of past glories.

Left The large and airy ex-LNER station at Preston (together with Liverpool Exchange) had the distinction of playing host to the very last regular steam working on BR, the 9.25pm service from Preston to Liverpool on 3 August 1968. Therefore even in the last months of steam traction it saw quite a lot of activity, as here on 26 February 1968 with Class '5' 4-6-0 No 45134 about to leave with a midday down parcels train.

Right On 18 August 1967 Class '9F' 2-10-0 No 92203 pauses in the rain at Preston station with a down ballast train.

Below Preston was always famous for its arrays of signals, and on 26 February 1968 4-6-0 No 44761 and an up coal train thread through the gantries at the southern end of the station.

Above I don't know whether you could exactly describe the former Lancashire & Yorkshire Railway (L&YR) and Great Northern Railway (GNR) joint station at Wakefield Kirkgate as large, but it had an overall roof and lots of steam activity even in 1966; as these next pictures show, all taken on 22 September 1966, there was also a good variety of locomotives. In the first ex-WD Class '8F' No 90617 pulls through the station with a northbound coal train.

Above right 'Britannia' 'Pacific' No 70026 *Polar Star* (its name now only painted on) arrives at Kirkgate with a van train from Lancashire to the West Riding. The whole area around Kirkgate station was controlled by semaphore signals, as this scene well shows.

Right Just before No 70026 arrived, 'Black Five' 4-6-0 No 45197 paused at the station with a Preston to Leeds parcels train. At the rear of the train is a Class 40 diesel with an eastbound train. Note the locomotive's shed code – 10D, Lostock Hall, Preston.

WD 2-8-0s pass at Kirkgate station. On the right is No 90649 with a northbound coal train, and running through the station is No 90625 on eastbound coal empties. Another van train occupies the westbound/northbound platform and the railway official is giving me a quizzical look! I have talked about the sight and sound of a large station, but what about that wonderful steam locomotive smell that lingered around such places!

The final scene at Wakefield Kirkgate shows a fine locomotive on a lowly task. One of Sir William Stanier's handsome-looking 'Jubilee' Class 4-6-0s, No 45593 *Kholapur*, runs eastwards out of the station with a ballast and track train. This locomotive is now preserved at Tyseley Railway Museum, and over the years has been a regular performer on main-line specials.

3. PASSENGER TRAINS AND SPECIALS

In the last few years of steam on BR, steam-hauled passenger trains were not very plentiful, mainly, of course, because diesel multiple units (DMUs) had taken over many local workings, and the Type 4 and 5 diesel locomotives had taken over much of the passenger work from an ageing fleet of express steam locomotives. One route where most of the working during 1966 remained steam turns was that from Manchester to Bangor and Holyhead, where many trains were still in the hands of ex-LMS and BR Standard Class '5MTs'.

In the first photograph, taken on the evening of 6 September 1966,

Standard Class '5' 4-6-0 No 73160, fitted with Caprotti valve gear, runs along the North Wales coast at Penmaenmawr with a Bangor to Manchester train.

The second view shows 4-6-0 No 73094 rounding the curve out of Conway station, heading for Manchester with an evening train from Bangor on 5 September.

Finally, 'Black Five' 4-6-0 No 45393 catches the evening sun as it heads west near Penmaenmawr with a late afternoon Manchester to Bangor train on 7 September.

If you asked most people over the age of 45 where they were on 30 July 1966, the day that England won the World Cup, they would probably be able to tell you. I certainly know because, as they say, I have the pictures to prove it! I was at Lea Road water troughs just to the east of Salwick station on the Preston to Blackpool line where, on a summer Saturday, you could still see a succession of steam-hauled holiday trains conveying people to and from the world-famous seaside resort of Blackpool. The day started cloudy but bright as I photographed 4-6-0 No 45107 running eastwards with a morning Blackpool to Manchester train.

By midday the sun had come out, and No 45420 was photographed heading over the troughs with another Blackpool-Manchester train (see also page 70).

Above Another route on which to see steam passenger workings in 1966 was the Bournemouth line of the Southern Region. On Good Friday 1966 (8 April) ex-SR 'West Country' Class 'Pacific' No 34036 *Westward Ho* speeds through Basing with a morning Waterloo to Bournemouth train.

Opposite One of the pleasures of visiting the ex-London & South Western Railway (LSWR) main line of the Southern Region was to see the 'Bournemouth Belle' Pullman train, which, even in 1966, was still steam-hauled. On 10 September ex-SR 'Merchant Navy' 'Pacific' No 35012 *United States Lines* rounds the curve near Pirbright Junction with the down 'Belle'. The other view shows a close-up of the Pullman carriages of the 'Bournemouth Belle' at Waterloo station on 5 June 1967. Note the advertisement for the Branksome Tower Hotel, at that time one of Bournemouth's finest.

Above Also in 1966 a route that saw quite a few steam-hauled passenger workings, especially on summer Saturdays, was the old Cambrian/GWR line from Shrewsbury to Machynlleth, then on to Aberystwyth in the south and Pwllheli in the north. On 9 July 1966 BR Standard Class '4MT' 2-6-0 No 76038 climbs the 1 in 100 gradient at Yockleton with the down 'Cambrian Coast Express'. *Ken Blocksidge, Roger Siviter collection*

Above right The route from Machynlleth to Shrewsbury involved the negotiation of Talerddig bank, which in places was as steep as 1 in 52. Standard Class '4MT' 4-6-0 No 75004 darkens the sky as it nears the summit of the bank with the Saturdays-only 10.55am Pwllheli to Birmingham train on 27 August 1966.

Right A pair of BR 'Mogul' 2-6-0s, Nos 76038 and 76047, hammer up the 1 in 52 on the same day; the train is the 10.30am Pwllheli to Paddington. These sturdy 2-6-0s were first introduced in 1953 and were all withdrawn by the end of 1967. Fortunately, three members of the class have survived in preservation.

Above The first picture in this book shows No 7029 on the 'Zulu' special of 4 March 1967, and the other special on that day was the 'Birkenhead Flyer', organised once again by Ian Allan and hauled by ex-GWR 'Castle' Class 4-6-0 No 4079 *Pendennis Castle*, famous for its exploits on the LNER during the 1925 locomotive exchanges. The special is seen here on the outward journey near Cosford, between Wolverhampton and Shrewsbury. This locomotive is currently in Western Australia, but it is understood that there are plans afoot to bring it home. 1t certainly would make a fine sight on the main line again.

Left On Sunday 21 August 1966 a special charter train was organised by the Altrinchamian Railway Excursion Society called the 'Holyhead & Brymbo Special'. This photograph shows ex-GWR 0-6-0 pannier tanks Nos 9610 and 9630 near Summer Hill on the Brymbo-Shotton leg of the excursion.

Right Nos 9630 and 9610 are seen once again as they propel a different special train out of Old Hill Tunnel (on the Halesowen branch) towards Old Hill before embarking on to a tour of the North Warwickshire line on 11 September 1966. This excursion was organised by the SLS (Midland) and was named 'Farewell to the GWR 0-6-0PTs'.

Even as late as 1967 there were still some named steam passenger workings, although perhaps not always carrying a headboard. One such working was the 'Lakes Express' (11.00am from Windermere for Euston), seen here departing from Oxenholme on 30 August 1967 behind ex-LMS Class '5' 4-6-0 No 45331.

Ex-LMS 'Black Five' 4-6-0 No 44775 shunts vans by platform 3 of Shrewsbury station on Saturday 7 May 1966.
Note the Gothic-style chimneys of the station buildings. *Ken Blocksidge, Roger Siviter collection*

On Saturday 3 September 1966 Ken and myself visited the former Great Central Railway line for the last day of working between London Marylebone and Rugby Central. The first view, taken near Charwelton just north of Woodford Halse, shows 4-6-0 No 44872 with the final 8.15am Nottingham Victoria to Marylebone train packed with enthusiasts.

In the early afternoon another Class '5' 4-6-0, this time No 45292, heads off Brackley Viaduct with the 10.57am Nottingham to Neasden Sidings parcels train. The viaduct was 320 feet long and had 22 arches;

it was dismantled in 1978. Brackley station was situated just north of the viaduct.

Also on that final Saturday the LCGB ran a Great Central tour. The special train started at Waterloo and ran to Nottingham Victoria and Sheffield Victoria, then returned to Marylebone. The train is seen here on the outward leg of the journey just south of Helmdon station in Northamptonshire, hauled by ex-SR 'Merchant Navy' 'Pacific' No 35030 *Elder Dempster Lines. Ken Blocksidge, Roger Siviter collection*

Ex-GWR Class '5600' '5MT' 0-6-2T No 6697 poses outside Croes Newydd shed on 7 May 1966. This locomotive and No 5605 (also shedded at Croes Newydd) were the last examples of these sturdy tank engines, introduced in 1924 for service in the Welsh valleys. Both locomotives were withdrawn a few days later on 21 May. However, No 6697 is preserved by the Great Western Society at Didcot. *Ken Blocksidge, Roger Siviter collection*

A trip to York on 1 May 1966 to see *Flying Scotsman* (see page 43) also meant an opportunity to visit York shed. Ex-LNER 'V2' Class 2-6-2 No 60824 and 'B1' 4-6-0 No 61238 (formerly *Leslie Runciman*) were photographed in the gloom of the large roundhouse, which is now home to the National Railway Museum. *Ken Blocksidge, Roger Siviter collection*

Above and above right Also in York shed yard on that day were ex-
NER Class 'J27' 0-6-0 No 65894, ex-LNER 'V2' 2-6-2 No 60886 and
an unidentified ex-LMS Class '4MT' 2-6-0. No 65894 is preserved by
the North Eastern Locomotive Group at the North Yorkshire Moors
Railway. In the second picture we see ex-LMS 'Jubilee' Class 4-6-0 No
45647 *Sturdee. Ken Blocksidge, Roger Siviter collection*

Right Ex-Midland Railway Class '4F' 0-6-0 No 44422 awaits its
fate at Barry scrapyard on 8 May 1966. Happily, this locomotive was
saved from the torch, being preserved by the North Staffordshire
Railway Society at Cheddleton. At the rear of No 44422 is '4F' No
44123, another survivor, now preserved on the Mid Hants Railway.
Ken Blocksidge, Roger Siviter collection

In the summer of 1966 the York-Bournemouth trains were still steam-hauled between Banbury and the South Coast. On Saturday 13 August BR Standard Class '5MT' 4-6-0 No 73093 speeds over Aynho water troughs with the Bournemouth-bound train; note the Southern Region headcode. Aynho troughs, situated 4 miles south of Banbury, were among the last in use in the country.

The other two views at Aynho were also taken on 13 August and show 4-6-0 No 45051 on a northbound ore train, and No 44942 on the Bournemouth-York train. Unlike the up train, No 44942 does not carry a Southern headcode, but the usual express code of two lamps, one on each end of the buffer beam. The 'Black Five' will come off at Banbury and be replaced by a Brush Type 4 diesel for the rest of the journey to York. *Ken Blocksidge, Roger Siviter collection*

By 1966 Woodham's scrapyard at Barry, South Wales, was full of condemned locomotives, and on Sunday 8 May Ken and I decided to have a look round. Most of the engines were ex-GWR and SR types, with one or two ex-LMS types (see also the picture on page vii). The first two pictures opposite show ex-SR 'U' Class 2-6-0 No 31618 and ex-LMS Fairburn Class '4MT' 2-6-4T No 42247.

The three views on this page show ex-SR Class 'S15' 4-6-0 No 30506, ex-GWR '43XX' Class 2-6-0 No 5322 and ex-GWR

'Castle' Class 4-6-0 No 7027 *Thornbury Castle*. With the exception of No 42247, all the locomotives pictured here have been preserved, No 31618 by the Bluebell Railway, No 30506 by the Mid Hants Railway, No 5322 by the GW Society at Didcot, and No 7027 by the Tyseley Railway Museum. Obviously much credit must go to the enthusiasts who preserved the engines, but also some must be given to the late Dai Woodham MBE, who owned the yard and gave much encouragement to the enthusiasts. *Ken Blocksidge, Roger Siviter collection*

Two views of Nine Elms shed (70A) on Whit Sunday, 29 May 1966, showing Class 'Q1' 0-6-0 No 33006 and unrebuilt 'West Country' Class 'Pacific' No 34015 *Exmouth*. *Ken Blocksidge, Roger Siviter collection*

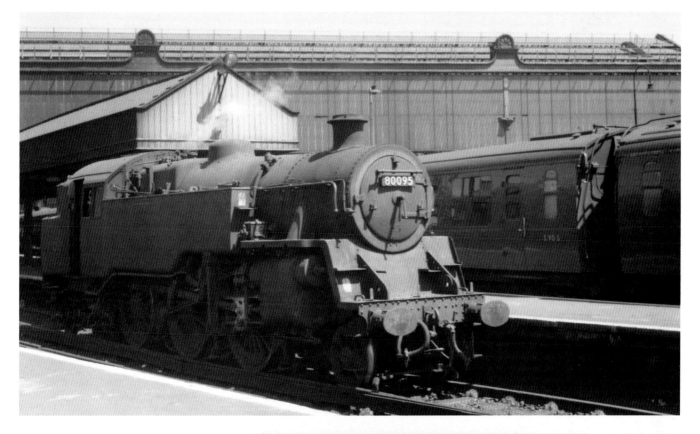

Earlier on that Whit Sunday Ken and I visited Waterloo station, where we saw BR Standard Class '4MT' No 80095 on station pilot duties, and 'Merchant Navy' 'Pacific' No 35012 *United States Lines* waiting to depart with the 'Bournemouth Belle' Pullman train. *Ken Blocksidge, Roger Siviter collection*

Left On 28 December 1965 ex-GWR '5700' Class 0-6-0PT No 9613 is caught by the camera outside Stourbridge shed. Although these pannier tanks' days were numbered, there were still a few allocated to Stourbridge shed for local trip working and shunting duties, and some of them lasted until the shed closed in July 1966. *Ken Blocksidge, Roger Siviter collection*

Below Also on 28 December 1965 we visited Oxley shed at Wolverhampton, where a pair of ex-GWR 'Grange' Class 4-6-0s, Nos 6871 (formerly *Bourton Grange*) and 6831 (formerly *Bearley Grange*) were in the shed yard, having been withdrawn from service the previous October. It was said that the 'Granges', together with the '47XX' 2-8-0s, were the finest GWR engines ever built, but sadly neither of these popular classes survived into preservation. Note the different-sized tenders. *Ken Blocksidge, Roger Siviter collection*

Above On the same morning at Oxley, Class '5' 4-6-0 No 44965 is being prepared for a day's work. *Ken Blocksidge, Roger Siviter collection*

Right Originally a Perth (63A) engine, Class '5' 4-6-0 No 45473 seems to have strayed a long way from home, being photographed on Bournemouth shed (71B) at the end of July 1966. On the left, in the original BR green livery, is Drewry 0-6-0 diesel shunter No D2275, complete with the BR emblem. *Ken Blocksidge, Roger Siviter collection*

On 11 September 1966 the SLS organised a 'Farewell to the GWR 0-6-0PTs' railtour (see also the picture on page 63). Nos 9630 and 9610 hurry down the North Warwickshire line near Woodend with the Stratford-upon-Avon leg of the tour. *Ken Blocksidge, Roger Siviter collection*

The 'Cambrian Coast Express' remained steam-hauled until the end of the Paddington through workings on 4 March 1967. From 1966 until the end it was hauled by BR Standard locomotives, and on 23 April 1966 Class '4MT' 4-6-0 No 75012 pulls out of Shrewsbury station with the down service. *Ken Blocksidge, Roger Siviter collection*

On a wet Thursday 7 April 1966, very grimy BR Standard Class '4MT' 4-6-0 No 75074 pulls into Basingstoke station at 5.00pm with a local train from Salisbury. This locomotive was built in 1955 and fitted with a double chimney in 1957, being withdrawn from service in July 1967.

This page These two views were taken just west of Brockenhurst on the evening of 22 July 1966. The first shows BR Standard Class '4' 2-6-0 No 76033 with a down local train from Southampton to Bournemouth.

In the second picture we see ex-SR 'Merchant Navy' 'Pacific' No 35029 *Ellerman Lines* with a teatime Waterloo to Bournemouth train. The edge of the New Forest provides a backdrop for both pictures, while out of sight just below the top of the cutting on the right-hand side is the branch line to Lymington, which leaves the main line at Brockenhurst.

Opposite Still on the Southern, this time near Pirbright Junction, we see unrebuilt 'Battle of Britain' 'Pacific' No 34057 *Biggin Hill* heads for Southampton with a midday train from Waterloo on 10 September 1966.

Another unrebuilt 'Pacific', this time 'West Country' No 34002 *Salisbury* approaching Catesby Tunnel near Charwelton on 13 August 1966. The train is the outward leg of the RCTS 'Great Central Railtour' from Waterloo to Sheffield via GCR lines (see also the picture on page 14).

Above left Ex-SR 'Merchant Navy' 'Pacific' No 35030 *Elder Dempster Lines* thunders through Basingstoke with a Waterloo-Bournemouth train on the evening of 7 April 1966.

Left BR Standard 4-6-0 No 75016 pulls out of bay platform number 1 at Shrewsbury on 25 October 1966 in preparation to work the down 'Cambrian Coast Express' which has just arrived at Shrewsbury's platform number 4 from Paddington, hauled by a Brush Type 4 diesel-electric locomotive. The train will depart for Machynlleth and the Cambrian coast at 2.15pm. In the centre background of the picture is Laura's Tower, part of Shrewsbury Castle.

Above Another view of Basingstoke on 7 April 1966, as 'Battle of Britain' 'Pacific' No 34052 *Lord Dowding* arrives with a down Exeter train with the headcode 'SPL2'. By this time steam had supposedly finished west of Salisbury, but it looks as though one or two workings were still running through to Exeter.

We finish this section on steam-hauled passenger trains with another two views taken at water troughs. In the first, ex-LMS 'Jubilee' Class 4-6-0 No 45627 *Sierra Leone* speeds over the troughs at Lea Road on the Preston-Blackpool line with a midday Leeds/Bradford to Blackpool train on 30 July 1966.

One of the other sets of water troughs still in action was on the ex-GWR Paddington-Birmingham line at Aynho, just south of Banbury. On 13 August 1966 Class '5' 4-6-0 No 44780 runs over the troughs with a southbound troop train. The spire of Kings Sutton church can be seen on the horizon, a familiar sight to today's photographers.

4. ON SHED

Standard Class '4MT' 2-6-0 No 76088 stands outside Croes Newydd shed (6C) at Wrexham
on the afternoon of 13 March 1967. The shed closed on 5 June of that year.

This page There is an atmosphere about the interior of a steam shed that is all its own. Light and shade seem to be everywhere, as I hope these two pictures illustrate. In the first immaculate Class '5' 4-6-0 No 44865 poses inside Banbury shed on Saturday 26 February 1966, while the second shows Oxley shed, Wolverhampton. Although Wolverhampton Stafford Road shed had closed by 1966, Oxley, the other ex-GWR shed, which mainly housed goods locomotives, was still open, and on 14 May 1966 was home to ex-GWR 0-6-0PT No 3605.

Right Reflections at Lostock Hall shed (Preston) on 25 February 1968. '8F' 2-8-0 No 48253 is surrounded by Class '5' 4-6-0s including, on the left, No 45345, which is being prepared to take out the 5.52pm Preston to Liverpool train.

Above left Stoke shed on the evening of 24 April 1966. From left to right the locomotives are 4-6-0s Nos 45284 and 44868, and 2-6-0 No 43018.

Above Sunset at Croes Newydd shed on 13 March 1967, with the rear of 2-6-0 No 76088.

Left Colwick shed (Nottingham) on the late afternoon on 20 March 1966, with, from left to right, 'Black Five' 4-6-0 No 44847 and '8F' 2-8-0 Nos 48361 and 48380.

On 18 November 1967 BR Standard Class '5' 4-6-0 No 73128 (fitted with Caprotti valve gear) receives routine maintenance work at Manchester's Patricroft shed. On the right is Standard 4-6-0 No 73053. No 73128 was withdrawn from service in May 1968, while No 73053 had gone by March of that year.

Another view at Patricroft shed, this time on 1 June 1968, with ex-LMS Class '5' 4-6-0s Nos 45055 and 44777.
By the end of the month this shed would be closed, together with those at Newton Heath and Bolton.

Tyseley shed, like many former Western Region sheds in the West Midlands area, had as a result of boundary changes been taken over by the London Midland Region; Tyseley 84E thus became Tyseley 2A. By the beginning of 1966 its locomotive allocation, apart from a few pannier tanks, No 7029 *Clun Castle* and 2-6-2 No 4176, was a mixture of former LMS Class '5' 4-6-0s, '8F' 2-8-0s, '2MT' 2-6-0s and a selection of BR Standard classes, as this picture taken on Sunday 15 May 1966 shows. Clustered round one of the two 65-foot turntables that were housed in the large shed are '9F' 2-10-0 No 92002 and 4-6-0s Nos 44780, 44661 and 45287.

Salisbury was always a Southern Region shed, although its number changed from 72B to 70E. It always had an allocation of ex-SR 'Pacifics', and was noted for turning out smart locomotives. On the morning of 7 April 1966 a very clean-looking rebuilt 'West Country' 4-6-2, No 34100 *Appledore*, is seen on Salisbury shed with Standard '4MT' 2-6-0 No 76012 on the left.

This page Shed yards were fascinating places where there were always locomotives being 'fed and watered' and, of course, turned. This was the scene at Rose Grove shed (Burnley) on 19 July 1968 – within days of the end of steam – as '8F' 2-8-0 No 48723 prepares to go on to the vacuum-powered turntable. 'Black Fives' and other '8Fs' await their fate in the shed yard.

Over two years earlier, on 1 May 1966, ex-LNER 'A3' 'Pacific' No 4472 *Flying Scotsman* runs on to the turntable at York shed to be turned in readiness for its return journey to King's Cross (see the picture on page 43). Looking on are Brush Type 4 diesel-electric No D1815 in two-tone green livery, and an unidentified 'Peak' Class locomotive.

Right 'Open wide, please' could well be the title of this picture of BR Standard Class '4' 2-6-0 No 76040 as it has its smokebox cleaned out at Croes Newydd shed on 13 March 1967.

Carnforth shed, together with Rose Grove and Lostock Hall, lasted until the end of steam, and even in the last few weeks Carnforth still had an allocation of 31 locomotives, with Rose Grove having 33 and Lostock Hall 27. On 16 April 1968 Standard Class '4MT' 4-6-0 No 75048 and 'Black Five' 4-6-0 No 45394 pose outside the shed.

In 1966 Croes Newydd shed still had an allocation of ex-GWR 0-6-0 pannier tanks, including No 9610 (with cabside GWR number plate), seen here inside the roundhouse on 7 May 1966. On the left can just be seen 0-6-0PT No1638.

Above Another feature of the locomotive shed was the coaling tower. Some were very high and probably became landmarks in their areas. One such tall tower was at Stoke shed, and nestling beneath this symbol of the steam age on 24 April 1966 are 4-6-0 No 45060 and a brace of '9F' 2-10-0s, Nos 92101 and 92102.

Left Ex-LMS 4-6-0 No 45345 is being prepared at Lostock Hall shed on 25 February 1968 prior to running to Preston station to work the 5.52pm to Liverpool.

Left Another high coaling tower was located at Bolton shed, seen here on 6 June 1968, a few weeks before closure. '8F' 2-8-0 No 48392 completes this twilight scene.

Above Winter snow returned on 2 April 1966 as Ken Blocksidge and myself finished our week's bash in the North of England. After visiting Leeds Central station, among others (see the pictures on pages 46 and 47), we went over to Farnley Junction shed (55C) just west of Leeds, where ex-LMS Jubilee 4-6-0 No 45581 *Bihar and Orissa* presents a lonely picture as is it coaled up on that bleak day. *Ken Blocksidge, Roger Siviter collection*

Right Towards the end of that snowy day we visited Wakefield shed, where ex-LNER Class 'B1' 4-6-0 No 61024 in seen in the shed yard. On the right is an ex-WD 2-8-0.

Left In steam's final years you would occasionally hear of an unusual working. By the autumn of 1966 ex-Midland Railway 'Jinty' 0-6-0 tanks were very thin on the ground, so when I heard on the 'grapevine' that a member of that class had been transferred to Croes Newydd shed to work the shed yard, as soon as I could I drove there from the Birmingham area, hoping to catch the 0-6-0T in action. I was not to be disappointed, and photographed No 47391 shunting the shed's coaling on a rather dismal morning on 4 October 1966. I was only just

in time, for No 47391 and the few remaining members of the class, which had originally numbered over 400, had all been withdrawn by the beginning of November 1966.

Above Although the sun is not shining, these two ex-LMS stalwart locomotives, Class '5' 4-6-0 No 44661 and '8F' 2-8-0 No 48061, seem to be smiling at the camera as they stand outside Banbury shed on 13 August 1966. The shed closed a few months later on 30 October.

Below and right The large shed at York (which now forms part of the National Railway Museum) was always a pleasure to visit. On Sunday 1 May 1966 ex-LNER Class 'B1' 4-6-0 No 61019 is seen at rest in the shed, while clustered round the turntable on the same day are ex-LMS Class '4MT' 2-6-0 No 43071, and ex-LNER locomotives 'B1' 4-6-0 No 61019, seen in the previous photograph, and 'K1' 2-6-0 No 62046.

Below The last ex-LNER Class A1 'Pacific' in service was No 60145 (formerly *St Mungo*), seen here at Darlington shed on Friday 1 April 1966. This locomotive was withdrawn shortly afterwards on 19 June, leaving no members of this famous class in preservation. However, thanks to the efforts of the North Eastern Locomotive Preservation Group (NELPG) an 'A1' locomotive is now being built.

Above Class '4F' 0-6-0 No 44203, an ex-Midland Railway design, looks almost ghostly as it receives attention at Westhouses shed (16G) on 17 May 1966. This numerous class of locomotive (there were once nearly 600 in total) will all have been withdrawn by the following October.

Below The final picture in this section shows the delightful little shed at Middleton Top on the Cromford & High Peak Railway, with 'J94' 0-6-0ST No 68006 in residence on 17 May 1966. Note the beautifully ornate windows of this pre-Grouping shed.

5. NORTH OF THE BORDER

There was quite an abundance of steam at work in Scotland during the summer of 1966, with many workings of both passenger and freight trains and quite a variety of locomotives to be seen, especially ex- LNER engines and some pre-Grouping designs. Ex-North British/LNER Class 'J37' 0-6-0 No 64620 heads the daily 1.30pm Dundee to Montrose goods near Broughty Ferry on 17 June 1966.

After a morning's work shunting in the Fife coalfields, Standard Class '5MT' 4-6-0 No 73146 (fitted with Caprotti valve gear) and ex-WD '8F' 2-8-0 No 90534 and their respective brake-vans head towards Thornton Junction from the Cowdenbeath direction at lunchtime on Thursday 16 June 1966. The location is about 4 miles west of Thornton.

A contrast in Scottish stations. The first view was taken at Stanley Junction north of Perth, where the Highland line to Inverness left the Caledonian route to Aberdeen (via Forfar and Kinnaber Junction). The train just about to pass through the by now closed station is the 5.15pm Aberdeen to Glasgow service, hauled by ex-LNER 'A4' 'Pacific' No 60019 *Bittern*, on 20 June 1966.

The other view on the Caledonian line to Aberdeen, taken at Coupar Angus (16 miles north of Perth) at around 7.30pm on 15 June 1966, shows Class '5' 4-6-0 No 44998 pulling into the Caledonian station with the 7.00pm Perth to Aberdeen train, which, as can be seen, also carried vans. Note the busy looking goods yard, and what appears to be a large hotel. This Caledonian route has been closed for many years, the line from Stanley Junction to Forfar being the final section to close in 1982.

Ex-LMS 4-6-0 No 44720 and breakdown crane are pictured side by side in Perth shed on the evening of 18 June 1966.

On 13 June 1966 Ferryhill shed (Aberdeen) plays host to a 'Black Five' 4-6-0 and two of Sir Nigel Gresley's famous 'A4' 'Pacific' locomotives, No 60024 *Kingfisher* and No 60034 *Lord Faringdon*. The latter was withdrawn on 24 August 1966 and *Kingfisher*, together with No 60019 *Bittern* (another Ferryhill engine), during the following September. That was the end of the class on BR, but fortunately several examples have been preserved, including No 60019.

Above The WCML between Carlisle and Glasgow still saw a fair amount of steam activity in 1966, and on Friday 24 June of that year 'Britannia' 'Pacific' No 70036 *Boadicea* pounds up the 1 in 76 of Beattock bank with a Blackpool to Glasgow train. The location is near Greskine, halfway up the 10-mile climb.

Above right No 44879 leaves Dundee and runs along the banks of the River Tay with the 2.50pm Dundee to Perth goods on 22 June 1966.

Right It's late evening at Perth station on 16 June 1966, and ex-LMS Class '5' 4-6-0 No 44997 has just worked in with a local train from Aberdeen and will very shortly be going on to Perth shed to be serviced. The ex-LNER coach on the left is worthy of note.

Another Perth 'Black Five' 4-6-0, this time No 44998, pulls out of Perth on the morning of 18 June 1966 with the 9.50am local train to Aberdeen, once again also carrying a van; at that time most of the local trains between Perth and Aberdeen were 'mixed'. On the right is the Dewar whisky factory.

When I visited Scotland in June 1966 'A4' 'Pacifics' were regular performers on trains between Glasgow and Aberdeen, including the 5.15pm Aberdeen-Glasgow, seen here leaving Perth on 16 June with ex-LNER 4-6-2 No 60019 *Bittern* in charge. At that time another regular working was the 8.25am Glasgow-Aberdeen, while the 1.30pm Aberdeen-Glasgow service was often in the hands of 'A2' 'Pacific' No 60532 *Blue Peter*, now happily preserved.

Below and right 'A2' 'Pacific' *Blue Peter* was mentioned in the last caption, but at the time another member of the class could also be found, mostly at Dundee shed where it was a standby locomotive – No 60530 *Sayajirao*. The first two views here show the powerful locomotive as it languished at Dundee shed on the morning of 17 June 1966. It did work occasionally on the main line during that summer, but to most people's frustration it was nearly always on standby duty. *Sayajirao* was withdrawn from service in November 1966.

Right 'A4' 'Pacific' No 60034 *Lord Faringdon* is turned at Ferryhill prior to working out of Aberdeen with the 1.30pm to Glasgow on 14 June 1966.

Opposite Two views of 'A4' 'Pacific' No 60019 *Bittern* as it hurries through Gleneagles station on 18 June 1966 with the 'Grampian', the 5.15pm Aberdeen to Glasgow train. In the first view we can see the trackbed and loop platform used by the branch line to Crieff, which ran north-west out of the station, but had closed in 1965.

Above In the summer of 1966 another working that would often produce interesting locomotives was the 8.29am empty stock train from Dundee to Perth, seen here on 22 June 1966 about to cross the River Tay at Perth hauled by ex-LNER Class 'V2' 2-6-2 No 60813.

This locomotive was unique in that it was fitted with smoke deflectors, and had been withdrawn from service by the end of September 1966.

Below Former LNER Class 'A2' 'Pacific' No 60532 *Blue Peter* bursts out of Moncrieff Tunnel at Hilton Junction, just south of Perth, and takes the line to Stirling with the 1.30pm Aberdeen-Glasgow train on 20 June 1966. The other line leads to Bridge of Earn, where the Glenfarg route to Edinburgh (closed in 1970) parts company with the Ladybank line, which runs through the Kingdom of Fife, also to Edinburgh.

A more than common occurrence in steam days, No 60019 *Bittern* takes water at Perth while at the head of the down 'Grampian' on Friday 17 June 1966. The train left Glasgow Buchanan Street at 8.25am, arriving at Perth at 9.40am, leaving again at 9.43, thus allowing 3 minutes to take on passengers and water. Arrival in Aberdeen was scheduled for 11.25am, taking 3 hours for the 153-mile journey, which also included a stop at Forfar.

As a local train left Perth at 9.50am for Aberdeen, there was clearly no margin for error in these runs. The up 'Grampian', the 1.30pm from Aberdeen (with more stops), was allowed 4 hours for the run to Glasgow, but the 5.15pm Aberdeen to Glasgow train, as with the 8.25am ex-Glasgow, was required to do the journey in 3 hours.

One of Sir Nigel Gresley's Class 'J38' 0-6-0s, No 65914, trundles down the bank to Thornton Junction with a train of scrap metal from the Dunfermline area. The location is Cluny, near Bowhill, and the date is 16 June 1966.

6. DIESEL INVASION

Left With the advent of diesel traction on BR and the demise of steam, until purpose-built depots were ready for the new motive power, steam and diesel were usually to be found side by side at the old steam sheds. On 16 April 1968 an English Electric Type 4 (later Class 40) diesel-electric stands in Carnforth shed yard as Class '5' 4-6-0 No 45394 simmers outside the shed.

This page On 25 April 1968 Stockport Edgeley shed plays host to 4-6-0s Nos 44868 and 44871, 2-8-0s Nos 48170 and 48267, and a Sulzer Type 2 Bo-Bo diesel-electric locomotive. The second photograph is another view of Nos 48267 and 44868 at the shed on the same day, this time silhouetted against the setting sun. The electric catenary is a reminder of the other new form of motive power shortly to be in the ascendant.

Left Bolton shed on 6 June 1968, as a Type 2 diesel-electric mingles with the 'Black Fives' and '8Fs', among which are Nos 44947, 45073, 45290, 45318, 48337 and 48773. Note also in the background the distinctive shape of a Morris Minor and what looks like a Ford Anglia.

Right After showing steam and diesel together, the next few pictures show some of the diesel types of the period (many of which are now themselves vanished and the subject of preservation projects) at work, mainly at the end of BR steam and just after. The first scene, taken on 29 March 1966, shows Brush Type 4 No D1853 descending Shap bank near Scout Green box with the up 'Midday Scot'. Note the track maintenance men – no 'visivests' in those days!

Below One of the early DMUs, a Western Region three-car set, runs through Tyseley South junction with a down local service on the afternoon of 31 January 1966. The North Warwickshire line can be seen veering off to the right.

Steam has all but finished on the Southern Region as a Type 2 Sulzer diesel-electric (later known as Class 33), built by Birmingham Railway Carriage & Wagon Co, hurries down the old LSWR four-track main line near Basing with a mid-morning westbound passenger train on Sunday 2 July 1967. These locomotives were first introduced in 1958 and have only just finished work on BR; several examples remain in preservation.

The next five pictures show some of the types of diesel locomotives that were introduced in the late 1950s and early 1960s to replace the existing fleet of steam locomotives. All these classes had been withdrawn by the mid-1980s, but examples remain in preservation. Indeed, as you will see, the preserved English Electric 'Deltics' are now back on the main line, not only hauling special charters but also regular workings.

Above On 13 August 1983 Class 25/2 diesels Nos 25181 and 25229 (originally Nos D7531 and D7579) ease into Dovey Junction with the 0700 Shrewsbury to Aberystwyth summer Saturday train. These Sulzer Type 2 diesels were introduced in 1961 but were withdrawn by the mid-1980s. Among enthusiasts they were affectionately known as 'Rats'. The GWR bracket signal dominates this mid-Wales scene. *Christina Siviter*

The Type 4 'Peak' Class diesels were first introduced in 1959, and remained in service until around 1987. They could be found at work in many areas, especially the Midlands and the West Country, where they worked holiday trains from the North West and North East of England to the seaside resorts of Devon and Cornwall. No 45143 (originally D62) *5th Royal Inniskilling Dragoon Guards* pulls out of Exeter St David's passing one of the famous bracket signals on 7 July 1984 with the 0911 Manchester Piccadilly to Newquay train.

By 1985, with the construction of Exeter's new power box, the manual signal boxes and semaphores had been replaced. However, the West signal box, glimpsed here above the train, has been preserved and can now be seen in working order at Crewe Heritage Centre. *Christina Siviter*

Above One of the earliest diesel classes on BR (they first appeared in 1958) was the English Electric Type 4, later known as Class 40. Like the Class 25s they were withdrawn by the mid-1980s, and in their later years were often to be found on minor freight working, as shown here on 14 April 1983 with No 40177 (D377) passing Helsby Junction from Ellesmere Port with a short mixed goods train bound for the Manchester area. *Christina Siviter*

Left In the autumn of 1981, just prior to their withdrawal, the very popular 'Deltic' Class locomotives ran a series of 'Farewell' specials. On 24 October 1981 No 55015 (D9015) *Tulyar* prepares to leave platform 15 at York with the 'Deltic Salute' to Aberdeen, organised by the Deltic Preservation Society. These English Electric locomotives, with their 3,300bhp, were the most powerful diesels on BR when they were introduced in 1961. *Christina Siviter*

The previous picture showed a 'Deltic' in its later livery of BR blue. However, one of the preserved examples of the class, No D9000 (later 55022) *Royal Scots Grey*, is now turned out in the original BR livery of two-tone green. On 21 August 1999 No D9000 heads the 1210 Saturdays-only) Ramsgate to Birmingham New Street train near Kings Sutton, just south of Banbury. No D9000 was the regular locomotive used on this train throughout the summer timetable.

Left Littleton Colliery near Cannock is the setting on 23 October 1969 as *No 7*, a Hudswell Clarke 0-6-0ST built in 1943 (Works No 1752), shunts in the rear colliery yard.

Above Littleton Colliery's best-known locomotive was *Littleton No 5*, a large 0-6-0ST built by Manning Wardle in 1922 (Works No 2018), now happily preserved. Here it shunts wagons at Boscomoor sidings (situated between the colliery and the BR exchange sidings at Penkridge) on 5 September 1969.

Right Until the early 1970s Bowne & Shaw Ltd at Wirksworth Quarry in Derbyshire employed steam locomotives, including *Uppingham*, a Peckett 0-4-0ST built in 1912 (Works No 1257). On 14 April 1972 *Uppingham* shunts loaded wagons in the quarry yard. The quarry also had the distinction, at one time, of employing the oldest working steam locomotive, *Holwell No 3*, a Black Hawthorn 0-4-0ST built in 1873 (Works No 266), but by this date it was out of use.

Left On 10 April 1972 No S100, a Hudswell Clarke 0-6-0T of 1949 vintage (Works No 1822), propels another load up to the spoil tip at Peckfield Colliery near Micklefield in the NCB North Yorkshire area.

Below left Most collieries were set in rural areas, and Cadley Hill Colliery near Burton upon Trent was no exception. On 24 March 1972 Hunslet 0-6-0ST *Cadley Hill No 1* is in a sylvan setting, taking a load of empty wagons from the exchange sidings to the colliery.

Above right Steam working at Cadbury's factory at Bournville finished around the mid-1960s. However, one of their 0-4-0Ts, *No 1*, was preserved and is seen on 30 May 1966 at the Dowty factory sidings near Ashchurch. This locomotive was built by the Avonside Engine Co in 1925 (Works No 1977) with outside Walschaerts valve gear. *Ken Blocksidge, Roger Siviter collection*

Right *Austin 3*, a Hunslet 0-6-0ST built in 1937 (Works No 1814) is in fine external condition at the Austin Longbridge factory on 4 June 1966, although at the time it was not in use. *Ken Blocksidge, Roger Siviter collection*

Above Deep snow at West Cannock Colliery, Hednesford, as 0-6-0ST *Topham*, built by Bagnall in 1922 (Works No 2193), shunts the exchange sidings by the BR Walsall-Rugeley line on 7 January 1970. Note the LNWR-style lower-quadrant signal and signal box.

Above right At Mountain Ash on 25 October 1972 No 8, an 0-6-0ST originally built by Robert Stephenson & Hawthorns in 1944 (Works No 7139) and rebuilt by Hunslet in 1961 (Works No 3880), crosses the Afon Cynon and heads for the colliery with a load of coal from Deep Duffryn Washery.

Right *Sir John*, an Avonside 0-6-0ST originally built in 1914 (Works No 1680) and rebuilt by the same firm in 1929, is busy shunting at Mountain Ash on 12 March 1973. In the foreground are the remains of the platform of the long-closed GWR station.

The final set of colour pictures shows preserved locomotives at work on the main line over the last few years, and thanks should be given here to the many people who organise these trips, not least for the efforts of the Friends of the Main Line Steam Locomotive Operators (formerly SLOA), who have been involved in main-line steam running since the 1970s.

On 22 November 1997 steam returned to the famous Lickey bank after an absence of many years. The Bristol-Birmingham-Walsall special, hauled by LMS Stanier Class '5MT' 2-6-0 No 2968 and GWR Churchward Class '4MT' 2-6-0 No 7325, makes a fine sight as the locomotives storm up the Lickey near Pike's Pool on that lovely late autumn day.

West Highland reflections: LNER Gresley Class 'K4' 2-6-0 No 3442 *The Great Marquess* heads a Fort William to Mallaig train near Fassfern on 24 July 1989.

Steam on the Settle & Carlisle: Stanier LMS '7P' 'Princess Royal' Class 'Pacific' No 6201 *Princess Elizabeth* and a rake of maroon coaches head north near Eden Lacey with a Blackburn-Carlisle special on 25 July 1987. *Christina Siviter*

Above LNER 'Pacific' locomotives have always been popular motive power for special trains, especially over the S&C route with its stiff gradients. On the glorious evening of 16 May 1992 'A3' 'Pacific' *Flying Scotsman* approaches Ais Gill summit in fine style with a return Carlisle to Blackburn special.

Right After leaving Appleby on the S&C, southbound trains are faced with a stiff 18-mile climb up to Ais Gill summit, and on 6 March 1993 'A2' 'Pacific' *Blue Peter* pulls away from Appleby and heads for Ais Gill with a Carlisle-Bradford-Newcastle special.

Above left GWR 'King' Class 4-6-0 No 6024 *King Edward I* is back on its old stamping ground as it climbs Hatton Bank with a Didcot-Birmingham (Snow Hill)-Worcester (Shrub Hill) special on 10 January 1998.

Left On 31 August 1986 steam worked on the Far North route between Inverness and Helmsdale, but it was to be another 12 years before the next steam working, this time from Inverness to Wick and Thurso and return, over the weekend of 10/11 October 1998. The return working from Wick to Inverness is seen here just east of the

former Mound station (near Kirkton), once the junction for the branch to Dornoch, which closed in the early 1960s. The train is headed by ex-LMS '8F' 2-8-0 No 48151 *Gauge O Guild*. In the background is Loch Fleet.

Above In the autumn of 1986 steam returned to the former LSWR main line between Salisbury and Yeovil Junction. On 11 October SR 'Merchant Navy' 'Pacific' No 35028 *Clan Line* leaves Buckhorn Weston Tunnel, just west of Gillingham, and heads for Salisbury with a midday train from Yeovil Junction. *Christina Siviter*

On the evening of 12 April 1998 GWR '1400' Class 0-4-2T No 1450 races along by the Exe estuary near Starcross with the 1722 Exeter St David's to Newton Abbot train. This is one of a series of specials that were run over that Easter weekend, an event that was repeated in 1999. The 'Dawlish Donkeys' are also scheduled to run over Easter and during May in this Millennium year.

Above A typical Steam Age setting for a diesel-hauled train: Brush Type 4 diesel-electric No D1956 hurries over Dillicar water troughs, just south of Tebay in the Lune Valley, with an up freightliner train on the afternoon of 29 August 1967.

Below A Type 2 Sulzer diesel, No D7651 (later Class 25 No 25301), heads through Low Barn near Hoghton with a morning Preston to Blackburn van train on 6 June 1968.

When these next two pictures were taken at St Austell at around 2.00pm on Thursday 8 August 1968, steam had long ago finished in Cornwall, the last workings having been in 1964. Most of the main duties were taken over by 'Warships', or the more powerful 'Westerns', both with hydraulic transmission. In the first picture 'Western' No D1038 *Western Sovereign* has just arrived at St Austell station with a midday Penzance–Plymouth van train, while in the sidings next to the car transporter train is another unidentified 'Western' with the empty carriages for the car train. No D1038 is in maroon livery and the other in BR blue.

The second photograph, taken from the other side of the road bridge, gives a clearer view of the transporter train, with another unidentified diesel locomotive at its head, possibly a Type 2; the car transporter trains finished in the mid-1980s. Note the spur line at the end of the down platform, and also the 'Cornish Alps' (the china clay mounds) on the horizon. The 1960s cars and other vehicles, many of them now collectors' items, complete the scene.

Above An unidentified Type 4 'Peak' Class diesel-electric leaves Barnt Green and heads for Bromsgrove with a midday Birmingham to Bristol service on 13 May 1966. Steam workings finished in the Lickey Incline area in September 1964 with the closure of Bromsgrove shed; prior to that date Type 4 diesel locomotives had gradually been taking over the main-line passenger duties from ex-LMS 'Black Fives', 'Jubilees', 'Scots' and BR Standard engines.

Above right The 'Warship' Class diesel-hydraulics were first introduced in 1958 (three years before the 'Western' Class), but had a relatively short life, all having been withdrawn by 1972, although three examples of the class remain in preservation. They mainly worked the

former LSWR Waterloo to the West of England routes, and ex-GWR lines, especially in Devon and Cornwall. Here an unidentified member of the class is seen crossing St German's Viaduct on 30 July 1968 with a Penzance to Plymouth (mixed) local train.

Right On 25 July 1966 the Metro-Cammell 'Blue Pullman' train climbs smoothly up Hatton bank on its late afternoon journey from Paddington (4.50pm) to Birmingham Snow Hill and Wolverhampton Low Level station. These trains, which also ran on the Midland main line from St Pancras, were first introduced around 1960 and worked on the Western Region until 1973.

One of the most popular classes of diesels amongst enthusiasts are the powerful English Electric 'Deltic' locomotives, and with their impressive appearance and very loud exhaust sound it is easy to see why. During their BR lives they mainly worked out of King's Cross on the ECML, and on Sunday 1 May 1966 No D9004 *Queen's Own Highlander* was photographed near Escrick, south of York, with an afternoon King's Cross to Edinburgh train.

Instead of the two-tone green livery seen in the first picture, in the early 1970s the 'Deltics' were painted in the new BR blue livery and renumbered, as seen in the second view with No 55022 *Royal Scots Grey* (formerly D9000) as it poses in the depot yard at York on 24 May 1981.

That year was their last full year of operation, and on 23 May 1981 No 55019 *Royal Highland Fusilier* (formerly D9019) stands under the splendid roof at York station with the 1325 to King's Cross. Five examples of the class are preserved, and some have recently worked again on the main line hauling regular trains and charters.

7. CORNISH STEAM AND OTHER INDUSTRIALS

After the end of steam, and indeed during its final years, many enthusiasts became aware of the amount of steam traction still used in industry. From coal mines to quarries, car factories to docks, and many other industrial sites besides, there still seemed an abundance of steam at work. Granted, they were mainly tank locomotives often only to be seen in confined spaces, but nevertheless very photogenic and certainly worth recording.

By the summer of 1968 it had been over four years since there had been any steam activity on BR lines in Cornwall, but there were two contrasting dock areas where steam was still at work – Par docks, which shipped mainly china clay, and Falmouth docks, handling more general goods. Par docks employed two 0-4-0 saddle tanks, *Judy* and *Alfred*, both built by W. G. Bagnall, *Judy* in 1937 (Works No 2572) and *Alfred* in 1953 (Works No 3058).

These three pictures, the first two taken on 8 August 1968 and the last on 29 July, show *Judy* at work in and around the docks and, for good measure, posing by a contemporary lorry. Note the reduced height of the locomotive (for bridge clearance purposes), especially compared to the BR vans.

Some 30 miles south of Par is the deep-water port of Falmouth, complete with docks known as the Falmouth Docks & Engineering Co Ltd. There were three locomotives on this system; one was kept as a spare engine and the other two each worked one week on and one week off, to allow for maintenance. On 31 July 1968 No 5, an 0-6-0 saddle tank built by Hudswell Clarke (Works No 1632) in 1929, is seen shunting the docks. These two views, taken from the grounds of Falmouth Castle, give some idea of the size of the dockyard and port of Falmouth.

Above On the face of it, the motor industry and its allied trades would seem an unusual setting for steam locomotives, yet in Birmingham this was certainly the case, both at the Austin Motor Co at Longbridge and the Dunlop Rubber Co at 'Fort Dunlop', Castle Bromwich, where they were still using steam traction until the late 1960s. I visited 'Fort Dunlop' on 20 May 1969, where I took this picture of an 0-4-0ST (formerly known as *No 6*) built by Bagnall in 1941 (Works No 2648). The locomotive was undergoing a boiler test prior to resumption of work. During my visit I enquired how long they thought that steam would last at Dunlop, and was told that it had a long future. Within six months the rail network in the factory had been taken up and the locomotives disposed of!

Opposite Ken Blocksidge and myself visited the Austin Motor Co at Longbridge on Saturday morning, 4 June 1966. Like Dunlop it was not an easy place to visit, but thanks to Ken, who at the time worked for Morris Commercial, we were able to arrange an official visit.

The first picture shows *Austin 1*, an 0-6-0ST built by Kitson in 1932 (Works No 5459), shunting near to the then closed Longbridge station, which had served the branch from Halesowen and Old Hill. The station footbridge can be glimpsed under the old station buildings on the left. Note also the signal box.

The second scene shows *Austin 3*, another 0-6-0ST built by Hunslet in 1937 (Works No 1814), and the most recent of the steam fleet, the powerful-looking *Victor*, an outside-cylinder 0-6-0 ST built by Bagnall in 1951 (Works No 2996). In the distance, *Austin 1* is busy shunting.

Left The final view at the Austin factory on 4 June 1966 shows a front view of *Austin 1* shunting on the edge of the massive works complex.

Above In the 1960s the South Yorkshire area of the National Coal Board (NCB) still had many collieries that employed steam locomotives. One such was Maltby Main Colliery, just to the north-east of Sheffield. On the morning of 25 August 1967 *Rother Vale No 1*, an 0-6-0ST built by the Yorkshire Engine Co in 1929 (Works No 2240), is framed in the shed doorway.

Above Although Steetly Colliery was in Nottinghamshire, it was still in the NCB's South Yorkshire area. Seen outside the small locomotive shed at the colliery on 25 August 1967 is a Peckett outside-cylindered 0-4-0ST (Works No 2109), built in 1950.

Below Another area rich in coalfields and steam locomotives in the 1960s was the Kingdom of Fife, in eastern Scotland. On 20 June 1966 at Cardenden-Bowhill Coal Preparation Plant, 0-4-0ST *No 6*, built by Andrew Barclay in 1949 (Works No 2261), is busy shunting a lengthy rake of coal wagons. These Barclay 0-4-0 saddle tanks were affectionately known as 'Pugs'.

This next picture was taken at the Associated Portland Cement Manufacturers' (APCM) Oxford cement works at Shipton-on-Cherwell, Oxfordshire. By the time I arrived on 30 October 1969 steam had just finished working on a regular basis, and was used on standby only. Locomotive *№ 6 CFS*, an 0-4-0ST built by Robert Stephenson & Hawthorns in 1952 (Works No 7742), poses with a rake of wagons beside the impressive-looking works. Running along the back of the works is the former GWR Oxford to Worcester main line.

Left To obtain pictures of steam at work in very wintry conditions it usually helped if you lived reasonably near to steam locations. This was certainly the case in the late 1960s and early 1970s when I lived at Great Barr on the north-east edge of Birmingham, for the Cannock collieries were only a few miles away.

On 7 January 1970 Bagnall 0-6-0ST *Topham*, built in 1922 (Works No 2193), shunts in the exchange sidings at West Cannock Colliery, Hednesford, Staffordshire. In the background is the former LNWR line from Walsall to Rugeley (Trent Valley), which at the time was used as a freight-only route and for West Coast diversion trains, but which has now seen a return to passenger workings between Walsall and Rugeley.

Above Just over 12 months earlier, on New Year's Eve 1968, *Littleton No 6*, an 0-6-0ST built by Robert Stephenson & Hawthorns in 1945 (Works No 7292), shunts at Boscomoor sidings on the Littleton Colliery line from Penkridge to Littleton, just north of Cannock. Behind the locomotive is an ex-Southern Railway brake-van. Note the Pickford's lorry, the only vehicle on the newly opened section of the M6 between north Birmingham and Stafford, now regarded as one of the busiest stretches of motorway in Europe, a fact to which many readers will no doubt be able to bear witness!

Above Better weather for *Littleton No 6* as it crosses the Shropshire & Worcestershire Canal at Boscomoor, before passing under the virtually empty M6 with a load of empty wagons for Littleton Colliery from the exchange sidings with BR's Wolverhampton-Stafford line at Penkridge on 3 April 1969. Unlike West Cannock Colliery, where steam finished around 1970, Littleton, which had a fleet of six locomotives, employed steam until the early 1970s.

Opposite One of the Meccas for industrial steam was in the NCB's South Western Division, Aberdare area, at Mountain Ash, serving the local colliery, Deep Duffryn Washery and, just to the north of Mountain Ash, Aberaman Phurnacite Plant. There was an engine

shed at Mountain Ash that housed the locomotives, up to six at a time.

On a misty 12 March 1973 one of the best known of the 0-6-0 saddle tanks, *Sir John* (built by Avonside in 1914, Works No 1680), crosses the Afon Cynon after working at Deep Duffryn Washery. On the extreme left-hand side is the former Taff Vale Railway line to Aberdare, while on the right is the ex-GWR line to Aberaman and Aberdare.

In the second picture, taken on 26 October 1972, another of Mountain Ash's fleet of steam locomotives, *No 8*, an 0-6-0ST originally built by Robert Stephenson & Hawthorns in 1944 (Works No 7139), then rebuilt in 1961 by Hunslet (Works No 3880), takes a load of coal to the Washery. In the foreground is the Taff Vale line, and the GWR line is at the back of the train.

The electrification of Southern Region lines in Kent in 1961 more or less meant the end of steam working in the county. However, steam remained active on industrial lines in quarries, coalfields and at Bowaters paper mills at Sittingbourne, where two gauges were used, standard between Sittingbourne works and the exchange sidings with BR's Sheerness branch, and 2ft 6in gauge between the works and Ridham Dock. When I visited the system on 13 August 1969, steam on the standard gauge section had finished, but the narrow gauge was still active, closing a few weeks later on 4 October, when it was leased to the Locomotive Club of Great Britain (LCGB), and became known as the Sittingbourne & Kemsley Railway. The first view shows narrow gauge 0-6-2T *Conqueror* (built by Bagnall in 1922, Works No 2192) shunting a load of pulp wagons at Ridham Dock.

Above Although the standard gauge system at Sittingbourne had finished, I discovered *Pioneer II* outside the main works. It was a former South Eastern & Chatham Railway Wainwright Class 'P' 0-6-0T, BR No 31178, from a class introduced in 1909 for motor train working and light shunting work. The locomotive is now preserved on the Bluebell Railway at Sheffield Park.

Below The final scene shows another interesting narrow gauge locomotive – *Premier* – an 0-4-2ST built in 1905 (rebuilt in 1912) by Kerr Stuart, Works No 886. It is seen outside Bowaters works, pausing between shunting duties.

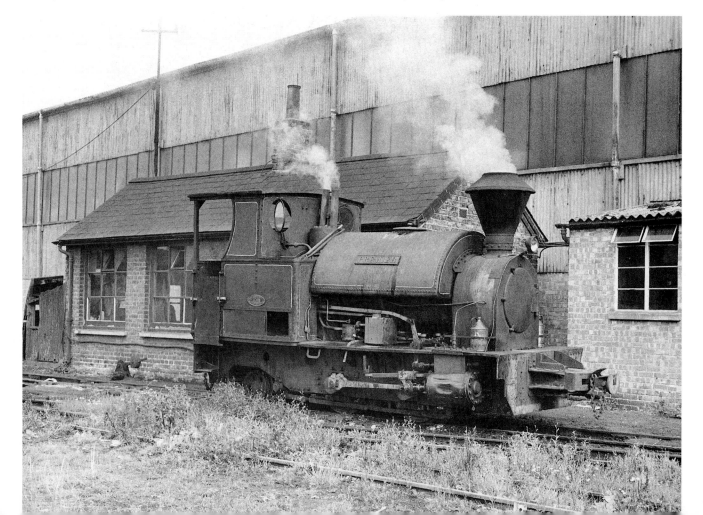

Some colliery systems were right next to the sea, as with Haig Colliery at Whitehaven in Cumberland. On the evening of 30 August 1973 *Repulse*, a Hunslet 0-6-0ST built in 1950 (Works No 3698), is shown first shunting the colliery yard. Turning round a few seconds later, it is seen on the edge of the nearby cliffs, below which is the Irish Sea.

Above Most colliery locomotives were saddle tanks, but at Fryston Colliery in the North Yorkshire area there worked a side tank locomotive. This engine was an 0-6-0T with outside cylinders, built by Hudswell Clarke in 1955 (Works No 1883) and named *Fryston No 2*. On 27 October 1971 it shunts on the exchange sidings outside the colliery near the BR Wakefield to York line. Note the industrial semaphore signals.

Left and right One of the last collieries in the East Midlands to see steam working was Cadley Hill Colliery near Burton upon Trent, where steam lasted until the mid-1970s. In the first photograph, taken on 23 November 1972, Bagnall 0-6-0ST *Empress* (built in 1944) takes a rest between shunting duties.

The second view is a conversation piece at Cadley Hill on 24 March 1972 between the driver of *Cadley Hill No 1*, an 0-6-0ST rebuilt from WD No 167 by Hunslet in 1961 (Works No 3877), and a colliery official. I paid many visits to the colliery around this time and was always warmly welcomed, and on one occasion had a footplate trip on *Empress*.

We leave the industrial scene with this 14 September 1970 view of a double signal on the former colliery line at
Rawnsley near Hednesford. In the distance can be seen the Rugeley transmitter on Cannock Chase.

8. MAIN-LINE STEAM TODAY

QUITE RECENTLY, while out at the lineside, a friend remarked to me that preserved steam had now been running on the main line longer than steam on British Railways. Although arguably never quite the same as in BR days, there are times, with certain trains and locations, when it gets very near the 'old days'. In this final section we see a small selection of the many thousands of special charters that have been run over the past years, and because it is impossible to cover the country in 20 or so pictures, I have confined the scenes to three areas, Scotland, the South West of England and the Settle & Carlisle route, which I think you will agree are very popular with enthusiasts.

One of the success stories of the past 15 years has been the Fort William to Mallaig trains, so what better way to start this section than to see LNER 'K4' Class 2-6-0 *The Great Marquess* crossing Loch nan Uamh Viaduct on the former North British/LNER route with the morning Fort William to Mallaig train on 25 July 1989.

Above This is the same train as in the last picture, photographed earlier on the first leg of the run between Fort William and Mallaig, climbing the 1 in 50 up to Glenfinnan station, where it will take water. On the right can be seen Glenfinnan Viaduct. The Gresley 'K4' is normally based on the Severn Valley Railway, but was originally preserved by Viscount Garnoch.

Below In July and August of 1992 a series of weekly steam specials was run between Aberdeen and Elgin in the North East of Scotland. On 23 August 'Black Five' 4-6-0 No 44871 threads the beautiful Aberdeenshire countryside as it heads for Elgin with the outward train from Aberdeen. The location is near to Oyne, about 4 miles to the west of Inverurie where the Great North of Scotland Railway had its Works. The line between Aberdeen and Keith was formerly GNSR and that from Keith to Elgin ex-Highland Railway.

This could certainly be a photograph from the summer of 1966 when No 60532 *Blue Peter* regularly ran on the 1.30pm Aberdeen–Glasgow train, but it is the late afternoon of 17 October 1993 and *Blue Peter* is heading out of Stirling with a Perth–Edinburgh train. This powerful LNER 'A2' 'Pacific' was introduced in 1947 and is the only member of the class to be preserved, being now very active on the main line.

We finish our Scottish journey with a view of probably the most famous railway bridge in the world, the Forth Bridge. In March 1990 the bridge celebrated its centenary; and in honour of the occasion two special trains were run, hauled by 'A4' 'Pacific' No 60009 *Union of South Africa*. The second run between Edinburgh and Perth heads north off the bridge on the afternoon of 4 March, while nestling below the massive structure is North Queensferry.

Above We now travel down to the South West of England for two views of the former LSWR West of England line between Salisbury and Exeter. On the evening of 10 June 1992 BR Standard Class '4' 4-6-0 No 75069 and SR 'West Country' 'Pacific' No 34027 *Taw Valley* climb the 1 in 100 out of Sherborne with a return trial train from Exeter to Salisbury. This train was run in preparation for a return to steam on the route, on 21 June 1992. In the background, to complete this Dorset scene, are the remains of the 12th-century Sherborne Old Castle, set on the edge of Sherborne Park.

Left A few days later, on 28 June 1992, No 75069 runs through Seaton Junction with the 1500 Exeter-Salisbury train. Although still known to enthusiasts as Seaton Junction, the branch line to Seaton closed in 1966; out of sight behind the photographer, the up platform and buildings still remain, now in private use.

After a look at the Southern in the South West we now turn our attention to the former GWR main line between Plymouth and Exeter. This is one of mine and, I am sure, many other enthusiasts' favourite stretches of main line, especially the 'sea wall' section through Dawlish. The first view shows 'King' Class 4-6-0 No 6024 *King Edward I* as it roars through Totnes station on the morning of 19 September 1998 with an Exeter to Penzance train – 'The Penzance Pirate' – organised by Pathfinder Tours. The train, having just conquered Dainton summit, now faces the climb up to Rattery, as steep as 1 in 46 in places. *King Edward I* was restored by the 6024 Preservation Society at Quainton Road in Buckinghamshire. Note the impressive chimney of the local dairy and creamery.

The 150th anniversary of the GWR was celebrated in 1985, and many special trains were run, including a return to steam on the Bristol-Exeter-Plymouth main line for the first time since the end of steam in the area in the mid-1960s. The outward trip from Bristol to Plymouth on Sunday 7 April was plagued with difficulties and poor weather for photography, but the return special on the following day ran smoothly, with good lighting. Here the return special approaches Shaldon Bridge at Teignmouth on 8 April, hauled by GWR 'Hall' Class 4-6-0 No 4930 *Hagley Hall* and 'Manor' Class 4-6-0 No 7819 *Hinton Manor*, both SVR locomotives.

Still in 1985, but this time on Sunday 14 July, GWR 'Castle' Class 4-6-0 No 5051 *Drysllwyn Castle* and *Hagley Hall* cross the harbour at Cockwood with the up 'Great Western Limited' from Newton Abbot to Bristol. No 5051 is preserved by the Great Western Society at Didcot. *Christina Siviter*

On 7 April 1998 GWR '14XX' Class 0-4-2T No 1450 (preserved by the Dart Valley Railway) ran a special trip from Taunton to Newton Abbot in preparation for the 'Dawlish Donkey' trains the following Easter weekend. No 1450 and its coach are pictured at Horse Cove, between Dawlish and Teignmouth, en route to Newton Abbot.

Steam returned to the Settle & Carlisle line during Easter 1978, and ever since there has been a steady stream of steam specials over this most popular of routes, and with its steep gradients and spectacular scenery it is easy to see why. LMS 'Princess Royal' 'Pacific'

No 46203 *Princess Margaret Rose* makes a fine sight as it heads out of Blea Moor Tunnel near Dent Head with a northbound 'Cumbrian Mountain Express' on 7 September 1991. This locomotive was preserved at the Midland Railway Trust at Butterley.

Another magnificently preserved 'Pacific' locomotive is the unique BR Class '8P' 4-6-2 No 71000 *Duke of Gloucester*, brought back to life by the Great Central Railway at Loughborough. No 71000 climbs up the Mallerstang valley towards Ais Gill with a southbound 'CME' on 1 June 1991.

Left An old water crane at Lazonby dominates the scene as LNER Gresley 'A4' 'Pacific' No 60009 *Union of South Africa* hurries south with a 'Cumbrian Mountain Express' on 24 April 1984, passing the former goods shed now used by a local bakery. The water crane was removed some years ago and is now at the end of the up platform at Appleby station.

Above During the first week of March 1993 a series of local specials were run from Carlisle to Kirkby Stephen, a distance of 42 miles. The locomotive used was BR Standard Class '4' 2-6-4T No 80080, seen here on 5 March at Kirkby Stephen having just arrived with the 1320 from Carlisle. With the signal box, goods shed, trackwork and semaphore signals, it is almost like a scene from the old steam days.

Right On 28 July 1990 Southern Railway 'King Arthur' Class 4-6-0 No 777 *Sir Lamiel* (minus smoke deflectors) runs through Dent station, at 1,155 feet the highest in England, with a northbound special. The various SR classes of steam locomotives, originally built to work on the arguably less arduous routes of the South and South West of England, have always performed remarkably well on the stiff grades of the S&C. This particular locomotive was restored by the Humberside Locomotive Preservation Group at Hull.

Above On 13 June 1992 No 60532 *Blue Peter* heads a northbound special through Sheriff's Brow, midway between Settle and Horton in Ribblesdale.

Below When it was at work on the main line between 1980 and 1996, the National Railway Museum's flagship locomotive, LMS 'Coronation' Class 'Pacific' No 46229 *Duchess of Hamilton*, was arguably the most popular of all the preserved locomotives. No 46229 heads off Ribblehead Viaduct with a southbound special on 11 May 1991.

Left On 26 April 1980 we see the rear of a southbound special as it heads through Dent hauled by LMS 'Jubilee' Class 4-6-0 No 5690 *Leander*, another SVR locomotive. A comparison with the photograph of Dent station on page 155 shows that in 1980 the signal box and semaphore signals were still in place and in use. The Morris Minor Traveller and Austin 1800 also date the scene.

This page Our final two pictures are night shots at Carlisle Upperby, where steam locomotives used on the S&C were serviced. One of the regular locomotives of the early days, but now no longer on the main line, was SR 'Lord Nelson' Class 4-6-0 No 850 *Lord Nelson*, pictured at Upperby on 23 February 1984. No 850 is also an NRM locomotive.

One of the oldest locomotives to work on the S&C, and perhaps the most fitting, was the Midland Railway Class '4P' Compound No 1000; in their heyday these handsome 4-4-0s were regular performers on this former Midland Railway route. The date of this picture at Upperby depot is 11 February 1983.

INDEX